THE 5min
Magnetic MONEY
MANAGEMENT SYSTEM

A Pocket Guide To Help You Manage Your
Money with Confidence in Just 5min A Week
- EVEN IF You Have Irregular Income!

MIRIAM CASTILLA

PRAISE FOR THE MAGNETIC MONEY® SYSTEM

Miriam is the Queen of getting your dollar ducks in a row and your money mindset sorted so they are on the same page and working together for you and your success... the steps are simple, easy to follow and we have fun too, I promise!

Magnetic Money® has really been a game changer in my business and home. I can't recommend it highly enough.

~ Anna Mason

Money has always scared me and budgets have always scared me but this program has helped me ENJOY my money!

I really had a shitty relationship with money before and now I have a wonderful relationship.

~Alexis Fotaras

This program is totally priceless!!

It is amazing and one of the best programs I've been in! I now know how to work my finances and make my money work for me. I am super confident as my mindset has also shifted and my money story changed for the better!

Thank you Miriam!!

~ Caroline Power

Wooohooo! I have SAVINGS for the first time in 20 years & after decades of trying to sort my finances. And no money worries! Just a deep knowing that I'm sorted.

~ Helen Swindley

Miriam's work has completely transformed my relationship to money and therefore my business success. Setting up the right strategies and processes from the get-go actually meant that I could call in more money faster!!! BOOM!!

~ Tamala Ridge

Magnetic Money® Management System

MAGNETIC

The (5min) *Magnetic* MONEY® MANAGEMENT SYSTEM

A Pocket Guide To Help You Manage Your Money with Confidence in Just 5min A Week – EVEN IF You Have Irregular Income!

MIRIAM CASTILLA

Magnetic Money® Management System

Miriam Castilla is a seasoned Finance Professional and Hypnotherapist who has built several successful, award winning businesses.

Her simple & practical approach to money is all about 'marrying the magical with the practical'.

She has helped thousands of people overcome money shame and financial stress by showing them how to transform their relationship with money and take control of their finances.

Miriam is especially passionate about helping women in business break out of survival mode so they can embrace their value and make a meaningful impact with their work.

Miriam is the founder of the Magnetic Money® Coaching Academy and the Magnetic Money® Club where she supports members to create a truly rich life.

She joyfully lives in sunny Adelaide, South Australia

Other Works:

Today's Woman, Life Balance Secrets: Practical Tips & Tricks For Overcoming Stress Guilt & Overwhelm

THE (5min) MAGNETIC MONEY MANAGEMENT SYSTEM

A Pocket Guide to Help You Manage Your Money with Confidence in Just 5 minutes a Week - EVEN IF You Have Irregular Income!

by Miriam Castilla

Published by The Effectology Method Pty Ltd

PO Box 1794 Burnside SA 5066 AUSTRALIA

www.miriamcastilla.com

Copyright © 2023 Miriam Castilla

The moral rights of the author have been asserted

All rights reserved. No portion of this book may be reproduced or transmitted by any person or entity in any form or by any means, electronic or mechanical, including photocopying, recording, scanning, photographing or by any information storage or retrieval system, without prior permission in writing from the author

Paperback ISBN: 9798396220386

DEDICATION

To everyone who's ever battled to get their money organized –
even though nobody showed you how!

Magnetic Money® Management System

x

CONTENTS

WHO IS THIS BOOK FOR?	1
MY PROMISE TO YOU	3
WHO I AM & WHY I WROTE THIS BOOK	7
FURTHER RESOURCES & SUPPORT	13

PART 1 – BEFORE WE BEGIN   14

WHY BOTHER	15
BUDGETS SUCK	21
THE MAGNETIC MONEY® PHILOSOPHY	25
THE 5 COMMANDMENTS OF MAGNETIC MONEY® MANAGEMENT	29

PART 2 – YOUR 8 STEP MAGNETIC MONEY® MANAGEMENT SYSTEM   40

M is for Map it Out	41
A is for Adjust Course	55
G is for Get Clear	71
N is for New Target	83

E is for EASY	91
T is for TRACK	99
I is for ITERATE	105
C is for CELEBRATE	113

PART 3 – CREATE A TRULY RICH LIFE — 118

YOUR MONEY SYSTEM IN ACTION	119
NEXT STEPS	123
ABOUT THE AUTHOR	125
RESOURCES	129

Magnetic Money® Management System

WHO IS THIS BOOK FOR?

This book is for you if you want some practical ways to manage your finances so you can reduce debt, accumulate savings and get your money working for you.

You've probably tried a bunch of budgeting apps, courses, blogs and processes but they were too fiddly, time consuming, confusing or just plain boring.

Maybe you have a small business or a side hustle and your income is inconsistent – or you just don't fit the box in some other way.

You know how important a healthy money mindset is and you understand that taking great care of your money is critical to get ahead. The problem is that nobody ever showed you how.

You want to create financial stability and feel confident about your finances, but the idea of budgeting and micro-managing your money is about as appealing as a poke in the eye with a hot paperclip.

And if one more person tells you to 'live within your means' or 'tighten your belt', you're going to scream.

You just want some simple, practical steps to follow – and a system that's flexible enough for your unique situation and needs.

If the above resonates with you, this book is for you!

On the other hand, if you:

- like spending hours tallying receipts and counting every penny,

- plan to keep martyring yourself and miss out on fun in the name of making financial progress,

- want to keep taking on more debt without taking responsibility for your finances,

- are unwilling to commit some time and effort to putting a system in place, then spend 5 minutes a week managing it,

- have your business and personal finances sorted, know your financial priority and how to achieve it – and have plenty of fun money to spend without feeling guilty or worrying about the bills...

- Then this book is NOT for you!

MY PROMISE TO YOU

I spent years working hard, building my business as a single mum to secure financial stability for myself and my children.

So I get it.

Money is a big deal. And it often feels frustrating, confusing, overwhelming and downright scary.

For most of us, it's also a topic that's tinged with guilt and shame.

As kids we were told that money doesn't grow on trees, to not be greedy, that it must be 'nice for some' and basically that it's not ok to want or have lots of money!

And this leads to all sorts of unhealthy beliefs and money patterns that stop us from owning our worth, asking for money and growing our wealth.

In business, it shows up as undercharging, overdelivering, avoiding invoicing and not following up. As employees, we find ourselves underpaid and under-appreciated, unable to work up the courage to demand that long overdue pay rise.

We're clueless on how to manage our money, especially our

personal finances. And it's tempting to stick your head in the sand and reach for the credit card, yet again.

But you KNOW that's not going to end well!

You do desperately want to get your money sorted. You want to be able to relax, knowing that your debts are shrinking, savings are growing and that you can afford that massage - or holiday - worry and guilt-free.

But you don't have the time or energy to become a financial wiz. You don't want to spend hours setting up yet another app and you certainly don't want to be counting every penny!

So my promise to you is this:

Stick with me through this short pocket guide and I will show you a SIMPLE, PRACTICAL approach to help you organize and manage your money.

Once set up, it will only take you 5 minutes a week.

And it will work EVEN IF you have irregular income!

We will cover how to smooth your cash flow and distribute your income if you have a business or side hustle with inconsistent cash flow.

And if you don't have a business or side hustle, you can skip one step, focus on managing your personal finances and making your money work for you.

I will show you how to reduce your debts lightning fast and start saving more money – while still having fun money to spend!

We'll make sure your bills are being paid – without needing to micro-manage your money, count every penny or constantly update an app or check your banking.

The power of the **M – A – G – N – E – T – I – C** money management system lies in its utter simplicity. We do it all in 8 simple steps.

Along the way, you'll hear from people who are successfully using this system in their daily lives and the difference it's made for them.

These are people just like you. People who thought they just didn't 'get' money, that they were 'not good with it' or that no system out there would ever work for them.

But this system will work for ANYONE! And now it's your turn.

Magnetic Money® Management System

WHO I AM & WHY I WROTE THIS BOOK

My name is Miriam Castilla, and I am NOT a financial advisor.

See, the problem is that financial advisors are not ALLOWED to help you organize your personal finances (crazy, huh?) What they are allowed to do is give you advice on where and how to INVEST your money.

But what if you don't have several hundred thousand dollars to invest in the share market? What if you're just the average person? And what if you have irregular and inconsistent income from a side hustle or small business?

Who is going to show you what to do?

Your accountant is only interested in preparing your tax return and business financials.

Your bookkeeper (if you have one) just wants to reconcile & balance the business books.

And when you look up financial support services, they're designed for people dodging creditors, in severe financial distress or staring down the barrel of bankruptcy.

But you're just the average Josephine, trying to figure out how to best organize your money.

You buy books and read blogs on financial literacy – but they bang on about investment vehicles, retirement funds and other stuff you don't understand.

So you download budgeting apps – but they're too fiddly or confusing. And if you have inconsistent income? Forget it!

So you buy a money course, but it only talks about money mindset.

It seems like NOBODY can show you how to manage your money!

Your parents may have told you to 'save for a rainy day' and put money in the bank (where it is literally SHRINKING because standard interest rates don't even keep up with CPI!)

I bet they also modeled all kinds of other unhealthy and unhelpful attitudes about money.

You went from being a kid who never really had to think about money – to suddenly being an adult with rent to pay, credit cards to juggle, maybe even a car loan or mortgage – and somehow you're just expected to know what to do.

So you join the charade, pretending you know what you're doing, juggling your finances, robbing Peter to pay Paul and hoping it all works out in the end.

The truth is, we live in a world of silent money shame, where everyone is putting on a brave face and pretending they're ok.

For me, it all came to a head after my divorce.

I had left my engineering and corporate career to have children. And suddenly, I was a broke, single mum, trying to figure out how to pay the rent and take care of my kids.

I realized how utterly STUPID I had been about money. I'd spent my corporate income on my lovely lifestyle – expecting the money to just keep on flowing. And I never put anything aside just for me or just in case.

I was royally screwed. I had no savings, no furniture – nothing!

I was forced to go on welfare and find my way in a new career. I scrimped and saved, making every dollar count while I built a business that allowed me to work around my children.

I was constantly stressed about money and had a huge amount of money shame. I felt like I had 'Broke Single Mum' tattooed across my forehead.

My new business was in finance and quickly became a success story.

But it didn't take me long to notice that many of my clients suffered the same kind of guilt and shame that I had experienced as a broke, single mum.

But it wasn't because they were broke!

It was because they had NO IDEA how to manage their money. They were always winging it, constantly worrying about money and struggling to have calm conversations about it with their partners.

That's when I had a massive epiphany.

The amount of money you earn has nothing to do with your level of money stress!

In fact, those on higher incomes often suffered MORE financial stress. They had bigger debts and bigger commitments with private school fees and loans for luxury cars and homes. And they were running on a hamster wheel to keep the whole thing from collapsing.

Everyone seems to think the answer to their money problems is to 'make more money'.

But, spoiler alert! THAT'S NOT IT!

Because if your money patterns don't change first, more money will only create MORE money stress!

The REAL solution is learning how to manage your money and shift those unhealthy patterns.

This is how you achieve financial freedom and peace of mind.

I started showing clients how to manage their money. And the difference it made to their lives, their well-being and their finances was mind-blowing!

Because when you start taking good care of your money, your money starts taking good care of you.

But there's even more to it than that!

Because having money confidence shifts your money mindset and aligns you with the energy of abundance. It literally makes you more magnetic.

As a result, you not only transform your relationship with money, you transform your relationship with yourself!

And THAT is one of the most beautiful gifts that comes from learning how to confidently take care of your money.

That's why I wrote this book.

To help you and others say goodbye to money stress.

To teach you what we all should have been taught in school.

And to show you a simple, practical way to organize your money – EVEN and especially if you have irregular income.

So that you can clear your debts, grow your savings and spend money without guilt, fear or worry.

It's about creating a truly rich life – inside and out.

FURTHER RESOURCES & SUPPORT

The following are available to further support you on this journey.

Free Resources:

- Download your implementation checklist:
  www.miriamcastilla.com/checklist

- Handy income calculators:
  www.miriamcastilla.com/calculator

- Organize and tidy your banking workshop:
  www.miriamcastilla.com/freeworkshop

Want more support?

The Magnetic Money® Management Bootcamp workshop series was recorded live and helps you set up your money system step by step: www.miriamcastilla.com/bootcamp

The Magnetic Money® Club is a vibrant community with live group coaching & support. We help you transform your relationship with money inside & out: www.miriamcastilla.com/magnetic-money

Part 1

Before We Begin

WHY BOTHER

Let's be clear.

You will need to put some time and effort into getting your money system up and running.

However, the great news is that the Magnetic Money® Management System is a simple process. And this guide will walk you through it in small, practical steps.

You won't need to spend hours setting up software or a complicated app, only to ditch it and have it gather dust alongside all the other 'things that didn't work'.

There's no such thing as 1-size-fits-all when it comes to something as personal as your finances.

That's why everything you've ever tried has seemed so damn complicated – or like you're trying to squeeze yourself into someone else's box.

But the problem with NOT having a system at all is that you have to keep winging it and hoping for the best. And so the stress keeps on building.

It's like being on a ship at sea with no rudder. You have no idea where the current will take you. You could remain forever lost at sea – or run ashore on a cliff somewhere.

Without a system, you constantly worry about the future – not knowing how you'll ever manage to retire, or just be able to slow down a bit and stop hustling, feeling like you're constantly putting out fires.

Then there's the 'tighten your belt and live within your means' approach.

At face value, that seems like sensible advice.

But I bet you want more from life than living like a scrooge and having to always say no.

Because you have dreams and goals. BIG ONES! Things you want to achieve, do and experience. And crucially, you want PEACE OF MIND around your finances and not live in a perpetual state of fear around money anymore.

For that, you're going to need a plan – and a system to help you execute it!

That's how you'll free yourself from constantly checking your banking, shuffling money in circles and robbing Peter to pay Paul.

For those with irregular income, implementing a money system can seem impossible. And I get it – I have irregular income too!

It's easy to believe that you can't possibly plan your finances if you don't know how much money will be coming in.

But you can! As Dr Seuss said "you just have to know how!"

Almost every money system out there will tell you to split your income by percentages or set dollar amounts. But when your income fluctuates, that doesn't work!

So most people with inconsistent income just make it up as they go, and find themselves falling more and more behind.

And eventually, it will all catch up (like when the tax bill comes). And that's when things get ugly.

The bottom line is, you do need a system and a plan. One that actually works!

And you'll need to commit to putting it in place.

So take a moment to reflect... WHY will you bother doing this?

- What do you want?
- Where do you want your money to take you?
- How do you want to feel about your finances?
- What are you sick and tired of?

Being strongly connected to your WHY will help you get the job done.

Once you're set up, it only takes a joyful 5 minutes a week to manage your money.

In fact, you will look forward to these 5 minutes because you'll start to see things truly shifting.

So take a few moments to reflect on the bigger picture and connect to your why before you move on.

Notes

My Why:

What I'm sick of:

What I want:

More Notes:

Magnetic Money® Management System

BUDGETS SUCK

A quick word of warning – I can't stand the B word.

What we'll be doing together is much bigger and more powerful than a boring old budget.

You will be making a PLAN for your financial future. And then you'll set up a SYSTEM to implement that plan, which allows your money to grow and multiply – mostly on autopilot!

How freaking cool is that???

So in my world, we don't use the B word.

Here are some BIG distinctions between a budget and a money system:

1. Budgets are rigid, whereas a great money system gives you loads of FLEXIBILITY.

2. Budgets are about deprivation and 'tightening your belt', making you feel small and powerless. But a great money system is all about EMPOWERMENT.

3. Budgets are prone to blow-outs, which make you feel like a failure. A great money system, on the other hand, is about making PROGRESS and adjusting as you go.

4. Budgets foster a lack mentality, with a message that 'there's only so much to go around so we need to make it last'. A great money system however, fosters an ABUNDANCE MINDSET and helps you energetically align with more abundance.

5. Budgets are about limiting your spending and 'living within your means'. But a great money system helps you achieve your financial goals so you can EXPAND your means.

So forget about budgets!

If you want to achieve your financial goals, create financial security and freedom, you need a plan – and a system to execute it.

Bonus points if that system also fosters an abundance mindset and raises your vibration so that you become more magnetic.

Oh look!!!

That's EXACTLY what the Magnetic Money® Management System does!

What a blessed coincidence... ☺

Magnetic Money® Management System

THE MAGNETIC MONEY® PHILOSOPHY

The Magnetic Money® philosophy is simple:

Your relationship with money is complex and multi-faceted.

Without wanting to sound too woo-woo, you connect with money on the levels of body, mind and spirit.

How we feel about money, the way we think about money and what we actually do with our money are all interlinked and interrelated.

And each one impacts the others!

- The way you feel about money affects your ability to attract more money.

- Your money mindset, beliefs and stories allow you to hold onto more money.

- And your ability to manage it wisely makes your money grow and multiply.

I call this the Magnetic Money® Code:

But any system is only as strong as its weakest link!

That's why we take a holistic approach and in the Magnetic Money® Club, we focus on nurturing and transforming all THREE of these areas.

Unfortunately, people who understand the importance of mindset and energetic alignment often ignore the practical aspects.

Nobody taught them how to manage their money, so they lack money confidence. And feeling uncertain, unsure and uncomfortable around money makes it tempting to just avoid dealing with it altogether.

It's easy to blame a poor mindset, childhood programming and other factors outside your control, rather than pull on your big girl pants and admit that you're a bit afraid of money and feel like you don't know what you're doing.

But unless you learn how to master and manage your money, your mindset and energetic alignment will continue to suffer.

Because a lack of clarity and confidence breeds uncertainty. It makes you second guess and doubt everything. And this undermines your money mindset and your energetic alignment in a major way.

That's why your finances can never outperform your ability to manage your money!

The great news is that learning how to manage your money is not hard and does not take long.

ANYONE can do it!

You just need someone to show you.

In many ways, learning how to manage your money is the final frontier. It's the critical link that makes everything else fall into place.

It boosts your mindset, makes you feel abundant, raises your vibration and creates trust in your finances.

And because managing your money will only take you 5 minutes a week you'll be free to enjoy your new state of abundance and focus on the things that truly give you joy.

This is what we mean by creating a truly rich life.

THE 5 COMMANDMENTS OF MAGNETIC MONEY® MANAGEMENT

Before we get stuck in, let's cover some basics.

The Magnetic Money® Management System is deeply rooted in the Magnetic Money® philosophy.

This makes it unique and is why it works so well for those who feel like they've tried everything.

The Magnetic Money® Management System is based on sound financial principles.

However, we also consider the impact each step has on your money mindset AND your energetic relationship with money.

So we often do things a little differently, backwards even, to the more traditional methods.

Our golden rule is:

Your mindset and energetic relationship with money trumps everything else.

I could write a whole book about this, but for now, let's summarize it into 5 principles.

Treat these as your guiding light and you'll experience a magical transformation in your relationship with money – and your finances.

NUMBER 1: Base It On Reality, Not Theory (and ALWAYS always add a buffer!)

> *"Theory and practise sometimes clash. When that happens, theory loses – every single time"*
> *~ Linus Torlvads*

Most people create budgets and money systems based on theory and fantasy. So no wonder they fail!

In the Magnetic Money® Club, I recommend members track their spending for 30 days BEFORE putting their money system together.

This is a massive eye opener!

I won't be asking you to do that here, but I highly recommend using realistic figures and adding a healthy buffer.

Wanting to reach your goals as quickly as possible is admirable. More importantly though, we want your money system to be sustainable. We don't just want you to like it – we want you to LOVE IT!

Buffers prevent budget blow-outs (which make you feel like you're failing). They'll also give you enough wiggle room to allow for those inadvertent 'extras' you'll forget to include at the start.

And don't worry that your buffers will soak up too much money and keep you from your goals. We'll ensure that doesn't happen.

NUMBER 2: Every Dollar Needs a Job To Do – And a Place To Do It!

"Make your money work for you or you will always have to work for your money"
~ Marshall Sylver

A lack of CLARITY is the number 1 reason people fail at money management.

Vague goals like 'having spare money' or 'saving' will keep you stuck.

When you employ someone, you don't just tell them to 'help you in your business'.

You give them specific tasks and a place to perform them. Else they'll flounder and be of little value.

Your money is the same. Every dollar needs a clearly defined job and a clearly defined place to do it.

This creates clarity, avoids confusion and ensures you know where your money is and what it's doing at all times.

Some money will have the job of paying your bills, some will have the job of keeping your business running, some will have the job of paying your taxes and some of it will be 'fun money' - money whose job it is to show you a good time. You get to spend this money guilt-free, knowing everything else is taken care of.

This one seemingly small principle makes a massive difference in helping you succeed.

NUMBER 3: Make Compound Interest Work For You, Not Against You

> *"Compound Interest is the 8th Wonder of the World. He who understands it, earns it. He who doesn't, pays it." ~ Albert Einstein*

If you've ever had a maxed out credit card, you know what it's like to struggle against the power of compound interest.

Compound interest is when interest is accruing on your interest - and then interest accrues on the interest on the interest - and so on and so on.

When compound interest is working for you, it's your best friend in the world.

And when it's working against you, it can make your life hell.

But compound interest (just like money itself) is neither good nor bad. It just is.

It all comes down to YOU and how you choose to use it.

With debts like credit cards, compound interest is working against you.

Unless you pay off the balance in full, you will be charged interest. And unless you pay off the balance PLUS the interest charges, you will be charged interest on the interest.

The whole thing starts to snowball, which is why getting those cards under control can be so difficult.

There's nothing wrong with using credit cards, as long as you don't become a victim of compound interest. You can still use cards to accrue points and get other benefits (we do!) Just be sure to pay off the balance in full each month.

On the other hand, here's how to make money while you sleep:

Invest your money so compound interest starts working for you, giving you a return on the money invested (along with other returns such as capital growth, dividends etc.)

Compound interest is now working for you.

Imagine a family tree. Your money has babies and the babies have babies. And then the babies' babies have babies… and so on and so on.

That's why we talk about 'making money babies.' *(Cute, right…?)*

Every dollar earned is an extra dollar you can invest so it starts making more money babies – taking the pressure off YOU having to work for that money!

Eventually, the effect becomes exponential – it's like a runaway train and almost impossible to stop.

THIS is how and WHY the rich get richer!

So your job is to stop compound interest from working against you – and free up that money so you can invest it where compound interest is working FOR you.

Keep this in mind when we get to step G – choosing your micro goal and No.1 focus.

NUMBER 4: The Formula For Getting Rich

"There is a science of getting rich and it is an exact science" ~ Wallace D Wattles

I learnt this powerful and delightfully simple money principle from Bob Proctor many years ago.

This simple concept has the power to change the way you think about your finances forever, help you achieve your financial goals and create an abundant life.

Most people practice what we call 'The Formula For Staying Stuck'.

It goes like this:

INCOME – EXPENSES = SAVINGS

They take their income, deduct their expenses, then save what's left. Or rather, they TRY to save what's left. Because Pareto's Principle kicks in – usually in the form of lifestyle creep. Before you know it, all the money's gone and there's nothing left to save.

They end up going nowhere – no matter their level of income!

A simple way to fix this is by turning the formula around into 'The Formula For Getting Rich'.

It looks like this:

SAVINGS + EXPENSES = INCOME

This means that the FIRST THING you do is decide what you want in savings – the money whose JOB it will be to grow and multiply and help you create wealth and financial stability.

You then add your expenses to that figure.

This tells you the level of INCOME you need to achieve your goal.

And if there's an income gap, you get to make a plan on how to bridge it.

NUMBER 5: Focus on ONE Goal at a Time!

> *"Focus does not mean saying yes, it means saying NO"*
> *~ Steve Jobs*

Most people don't have any clear financial goals.

When extra money comes in, or they have a good month in business, they just spread it around.

They put some towards having fun, some towards debts and some towards their mortgage, investments or savings.

But the problem with that approach is you've spread it too thin and feel like you accomplished nothing. You've gone nowhere fast.

That's why you need ONE clear financial goal at a time.

We already talked about your big WHY. And I'm sure you want to achieve some big goals – clearing personal debt, paying off the house, buying a new property or retiring in France.

Those goals are great for inspiration and motivation, but to achieve them more easily, let's break them down into smaller, more achievable micro goals.

Your job is then to just focus on ONE of those micro goals at a time.

You'll be directing all spare cash towards it. Whether you have a great month in business, sell your lawnmower, get an unexpected inheritance or win the lottery; ALL spare money goes towards that one single goal.

This will help you achieve it lightning fast. You'll be able to tick it off the list and move onto the next goal!

You'll feel GREAT!

You'll be high fiving yourself and happy dancing down the street.

This will fuel your positive new attitude towards money and reinforce that you ARE succeeding. It raises your vibration, making you even more magnetic to money, abundance, and opportunities.

This is how you create a beautiful, positive cycle where your ability and confidence in managing your money helps you nurture an abundance mindset and makes you more magnetic.

It's the Magnetic Money® Code in action.

And it starts by focusing on ONE goal at a time and adhering to the above principles.

Part 2

Your 8 step Magnetic Money® Management System

The Magnetic Money™ System

The Magnetic Money System is a simple & flexible process designed to help entrepreneurs take control of their finances. It helps you smooth your cashflow and reach your financial goals, is easy to implement and completely customisable to your situation, goals & needs.

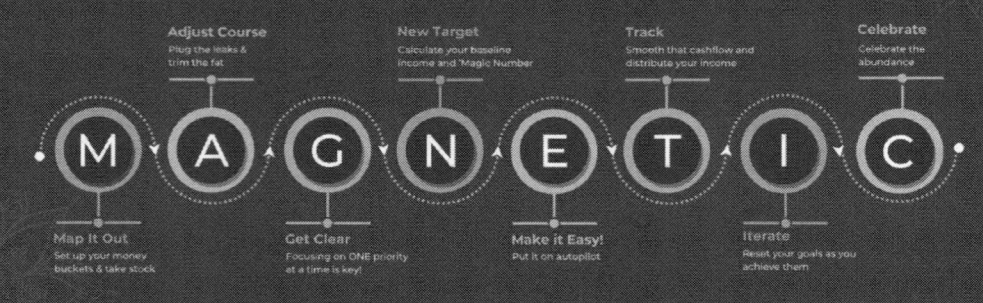

M — **Map It Out**: Set up your money buckets & take stock

A — **Adjust Course**: Plug the leaks & trim the fat

G — **Get Clear**: Focusing on ONE priority at a time is key!

N — **New Target**: Calculate your baseline income and 'Magic Number'

E — **Make it Easy!**: Put it on autopilot

T — **Track**: Smooth that cashflow and distribute your income

I — **Iterate**: Reset your goals as you achieve them

C — **Celebrate**: Celebrate the abundance

© miriamcastilla.com

M IS FOR MAP IT OUT

Set up your money buckets & take stock

"Being Organized is Being in Control"
~Edmund Burke

If you've ever organized your desk, wardrobe or any part of your life, you know that fabulous feeling of everything being in its place.

It allows you to deeply relax, because you know things are exactly where they need to be.

When it comes to money, this effect is exponentially!

Because the stress of:

- not knowing where to find the money to pay an unexpected bill
- feeling uncertain if you can afford things
- feeling guilty about spending money on a treat or luxury item
- seeing accounts overdrawn, credit cards maxed out or past due

... is intense!

So the very first step is to create some order.

You need a place for your money to live.

So you're clear on where the money is for this – and for that.

And so you can stop robbing Peter to pay Paul.

Organizing your money is a lot like organizing your wardrobe:

1. first you get your containers ready
2. then you pull everything out
3. you examine each item more closely

4. and if you decide to keep it, you tidy it up and put it in its proper place

5. So let's start by organizing the containers for your money.

Introducing the Magnetic Money® Bucket System:

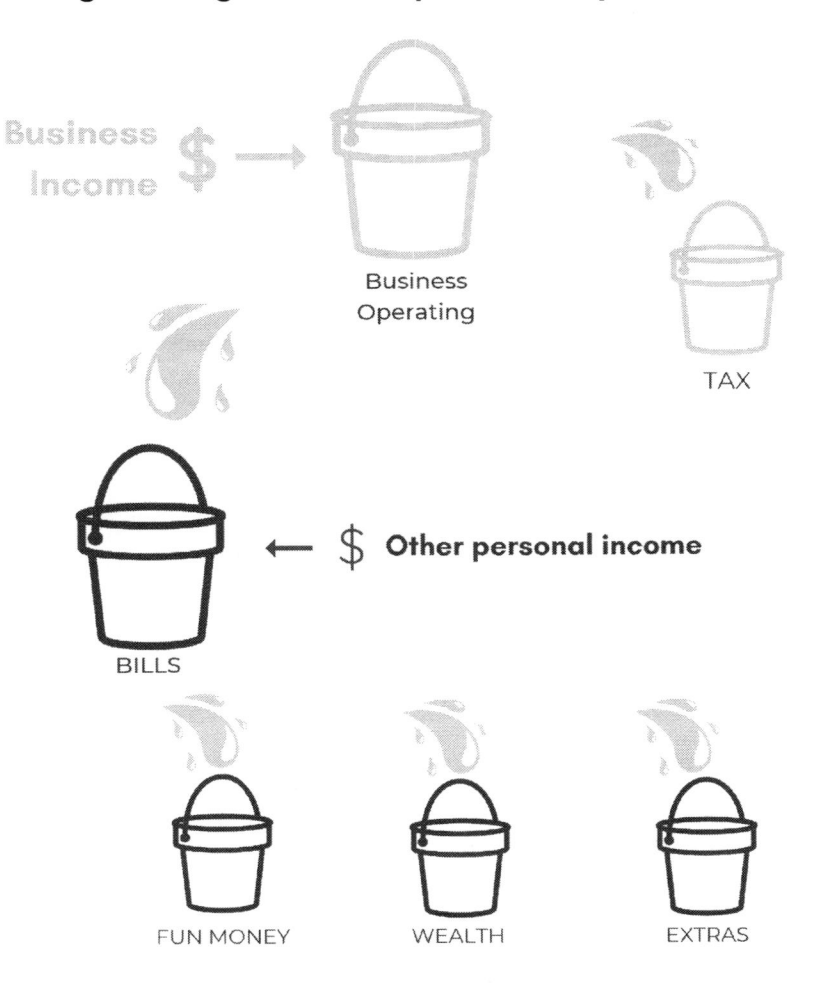

Business Income $ → Business Operating

TAX

← $ Other personal income

BILLS

FUN MONEY   WEALTH   EXTRAS

(if you don't have a business, ignore the top section)

The bucket system shows how your money should flow.

Your business generates income, pays its taxes and pays YOU.

It really only needs 2 accounts – one for each bucket, although many businesses choose to have more accounts in the operating bucket.

It's up to you – just do your best to keep things simple.

For your personal finances, you'll need money to pay the bills, spend on fun stuff and save for special events like holidays. You'll also want to pay down debt and create a level of wealth and financial security.

Each bucket represents one of these main PURPOSES.

And each bucket may contain 1 or more bank accounts.

For example, you might decide to have 1 bills account, but 2 fun money accounts – one for you and one for your partner. (which I highly recommend)

Depending on your financial situation and goals, your EXTRAS bucket may include several bank accounts. This is where you save for holidays, Christmas and birthday presents and other bigger ticket items such as furniture, weddings etc.

Your WEALTH bucket includes ALL your long term savings, your investment accounts (shares etc.) AND your debts (credit cards, personal and home loans etc.)

We'll go through this in more detail later.

KEY POINTS:

- If you have a business, you need SEPARATE business accounts.

- All business income flows into the business operating bucket.

- Your business sets money aside for tax.

- Your business also pays YOU.

- All personal income (including what your business pays you) flows into your personal BILLS bucket.

- Your bills bucket is the 'central nervous system' of your personal money management system.

- You pay your bills, and your business pays its bills – and never the twain shall meet.

- All fixed personal expenses (ie BILLS) are allocated to your bills bucket.

- All discretionary expenses (where you choose if, when & how much you spend) are allocated to the FUN bucket or the EXTRAS bucket.

TOP TIP: *When naming your bank accounts, make it specific and fun! Eg: instead of 'holiday', name the account '$10k Hawaii Fest' or 'Girls Vegas Junket'*

CASE STUDY

Magnetic Money changed my relationship with money in all areas of my life from my business to my relationship...everywhere!

I went from worrying about money allllll the time to trusting that there will always be enough.

At the time I came across Magnetic Money, there never seemed to be enough money in my life. I was always chasing my tail. I'd be able to accumulate a little – and then it would just go.

I spent a lot of energy and time stressing about money, worrying about money, where it was coming from, if there would be enough, etc. It took up so much of my time and energy; it was exhausting and definitely not fun. The stress also took a huge toll on my relationships and my health.

Setting up my money buckets allowed me to feel like I had some control over things.

My money buckets gave me direction, allowed me to clearly see what money I had available and more quickly than I thought possible, I began to see debt decrease!

It was when I saw money accumulating at the same time as I was paying down debt, that I knew money buckets would always be a thing in my world!

The other gift of the bucket system was that it allowed me to see where the gaps were in how I was managing my money. I could see where money was going that it didn't need to be and I became more aware of where and how I spent my money.

The buckets have honestly brought magic to my money. They have taken away the overwhelm around money in both my personal life and for my business. I can have conversations about money with my husband now without someone getting triggered. And worrying about money just isn't a thing anymore.

Today I'm debt free apart from my home loan!

I have a healthy buffer bucket and because I have my buckets set up, even if big expenses come up – or the bills arrive all at once – I know my buckets have my back and that there will always be enough.

Anna Mason
Clarity Coach
www.annamason.com.au

ACTION STEPS:

(a reminder a progress checklist is available here)

1. Set up your buckets and bank accounts.

2. Allocate income & expenses to each bucket & account.

3. Move items to correct accounts as required.

The following pages will help you map out your buckets and get clear on which expenses belong in which account.

Use the list provided as a starting guide, then check your bank accounts and keep adding to the list.

Magnetic Money® Management System

Notes

Allocate All Bank Accounts to a Bucket:

Business Operating

ACCOUNT DETAILS:
_____
_____
_____

ACCOUNT DETAILS:
_____
_____
_____

TAX

ACCOUNT DETAILS:
_____
_____
_____

ACCOUNT DETAILS:
_____
_____
_____

BILLS

ACCOUNT DETAILS:
_____
_____
_____

ACCOUNT DETAILS:
_____
_____
_____

FUN MONEY

ACCOUNT DETAILS:
_____
_____
_____

ACCOUNT DETAILS:
_____
_____
_____

ACCOUNT DETAILS:
_____
_____
_____

WEALTH

ACCOUNT DETAILS:
_____
_____
_____

ACCOUNT DETAILS:
_____
_____
_____

ACCOUNT DETAILS:
_____
_____
_____

EXTRAS

ACCOUNT DETAILS:
_____
_____
_____

ACCOUNT DETAILS:
_____
_____
_____

ACCOUNT DETAILS:
_____
_____
_____

Assign Income & Expenses to Correct Buckets:

Use the following as a prompt and add more items as you check through your bank accounts

ITEM	BIZ	PERSONAL BILLS	FUN	Debt/Wealth	Extras
Fun spending					
Alcohol					
Home Maintenance & Repairs					
Haircuts & personal care					
Kids' expenses					
Medical / Health					
Rent/Home Loan					
Groceries					
Utilities & Rates					
Personal Phone & Internet					
Fuel					
Insurances					
Car expenses					
Investment Property Expenses					
Investment funds					
Car Loan					
Personal Loan					
Credit/Store card 1					
Credit/Store card 2					
Savings for Buffer					
Occasions - Birthdays, Christmas					
Holidays & Travel					

More Notes

Magnetic Money® Management System

A IS FOR ADJUST COURSE

Plug the leaks & trim the fat

"Every dollar needs a job to do!"
~ Miriam Castilla

It's time to check:

1. Where is the road you're on taking you?

2. Are you driving with the brakes on or leaking precious fuel?

Let's go back to the formula for creating wealth.

SAVINGS + EXPENSES = INCOME

Every dollar you don't need for expenses, is a dollar that:

    a.   you didn't have to earn

    b.   can start making money babies for you

So let's plug the leaks and swap any expenses that don't serve you for ones that do – so that you can make more money babies, faster!

In the Magnetic Money® Club, I recommend members track their expenses manually for 30 days before moving forward.

This helps you get a handle on what you actually spend – rather than what you wish you spent. It's also a super interesting mindset exercise!

The purpose of tracking your spending isn't to make you feel bad – it's simply to ensure you start with accurate and realistic numbers, so that your new money plan will be sustainable.

We're not here to make you feel poor and restricted.

We want you to feel rich and abundant!

Now, you don't have to do 30 days of tracking, but I do encourage you to look through all your accounts carefully. Add up ALL your spending. We want to start with realistic figures to ensure your new money system is a roaring success.

Taking Stock:

Once you've identified each expense, you can see what it adds up to per year. This is usually quite an eye opener!

Then have an initial look at your bottom line.

Based on the expenses you've identified and your last 6 months average income – do you have a shortfall or surplus? *(don't panic if there's a shortfall – we will be taking care of that!)*

Just check in:

- Is there surplus or shortfall?
- How do you feel about it?
- Are you willing to do something about it?

Great – let's keep moving

First, you'll need to focus on eliminating any shortfall.

Then think about 'swapping expenses' – using your money in ways that serve you better.

> **TOP TIP:** *Leave plenty of wiggle room! Give yourself enough fun money so you feel abundant and proud of your financial boundaries. Don't be too stingy with yourself! Being able to spend fun money with confidence energetically aligns you with the vibration of abundance, making you magnetic to more.*
>
> *Also include a healthy buffer in your BILLS bucket to allow for unexpected expenses and any items you may have forgotten to cover. This will help you feel successful and empowered.*

Discretionary Spending (Fun & Extras):

These are expenses where you choose if, when & how much you spend.

Example: I need haircuts, but I can go to an expensive or more affordable hairdresser. I can go monthly or quarterly, or I can cut my own!

Helpful Hints:

1. When you review each expense, look at what it adds up to per year.

2. Then ask yourself questions like:

"Do I really NEED to spend this money – or do I just want to? And if so – WHY do I want to?"

"How do I feel about spending $5,000 a year on coffee outings? What if I chose to spend only half that & put the rest toward paying off the mortgage? Would I feel more empowered about my finances?"

Often, we say we NEED something when we really just want it. And that's ok, provided it's for a healthy reason.

Asking good questions will help you make sure you're not masking deeper issues with retail therapy. We all know that in the long run, that only makes you feel worse.

CASE STUDY

My story is probably a bit different as setting up my business didn't really work out.

But it has left me with another income stream and I also found out how to be happy in my day job.

By getting back into IT, I have been able to purchase 2 houses, and am pouring money into my self-managed retirement fund. I am so on track now, I am unstoppable!

But let me tell you about my day job:

I focused on how I wanted to feel at work. I wanted to laugh, to be surrounded by positive people and to feel like I had a seat at the table. Now I'm working for what is officially the '4th Best Place to work.' I permanently work from home, get paid a 6-figure sum and to tell jokes to our customers.

My boss's boss loves that I get to be me at work. When I first started, they sent me a bunch of goodies including cookies! I've been in customer meetings where they say "We love you, Di!".

My side hustle is still there. I have a number of money-making websites, which are mostly automated. I have plans to get them making even more money, and to take my IT job to 4 then 3 days a week.

I feel like I have the best of both worlds.

I still track my money and have my monthly money date to review my net wealth.

And I love the way I've so clearly named my accounts – Cash ($700), Bills ($400) and Wealth.

And I've just worked out that I'll be able to retire within the next 2 years!!!

Diana Gaskin
Senior Business Analyst

Fixed Expenses (Bills):

It's time to invest a little time and energy into reviewing fixed expenses & bills.

The cost of a fixed expense is never fixed!

So let's make sure you're not wasting money on things that no longer serve you, that you're getting good deals and not paying more than you need to be, just because you've neglected to review your bills.

Our Magnetic Money® members regularly save THOUSANDS of dollars a year – just by making the effort to review their fixed bills & expenses.

> **TOP TIP**: *The quickest & easiest way to save money: Google your current supplier's competitors. Then ask for a price match so you don't have to switch. Most of the time, they'll bend over backwards and start extending all that service you never got while you were blindly paying the bill. This includes loans, credit cards, mortgages. Be sure to review both interest rates & fees!*

Get creative and excited as you look for more ways to save money!

The possibilities are endless:

- shop at local markets to get fresher produce & support farmers
- buy dried produce in bulk, use glass jars & reduce waste
- get rid of the 2nd car or replace it with a scooter (we did!)
- buy recycled clothing and help save the environment

A NOTE ON TAX FOR SELF EMPLOYED INCOME:

You need to put money aside so your business (which may be you as a sole trader) can pay its tax bill.

Remember - you have a separate TAX bucket for this purpose (which usually consists of 1 bank account)

Each time you distribute income in later steps, you'll be putting aside a PERCENTAGE of your gross income for tax.

The percentage figure will depend on your unique circumstances.

I recommend checking with your accountant and looking back over your previous tax records so you come up with a number that will comfortably cover your tax liability.

Overestimate rather than underestimate so you have leftover bonus money at tax time – which is an awesome feeling!

KEY POINTS:

- Fixed expenses are never fixed.
- Delayed gratification builds wealth.
- Needs vs Wants: Why are you REALLY spending?
- Think about swapping expenses rather than 'missing out.'
- Feeling excited about your money choices makes you magnetic.
- Extra money is everywhere!
- Leave plenty of wiggle room so you feel abundant.

ACTION STEPS:

1. Revise your discretionary spending and adjust your allowances.
2. Shop around to save on fixed bills & expenses.

3. Review the cost of debts, ask for reduced rates & fees – or switch.

4. Keep a tally of your savings & get EXCITED!!!!

ADVANCED TIPS:

- Allow enough start-up funds in your bills bucket!

- check for expenses that will come up before you build up sufficient funds.

- use some of your savings as startup funds so those bills are covered.

- alternatively, create a temporary 'accelerator payment' to ensure you'll have enough funds available at the time. *(eg.. you have an annual subscription coming up in 3 months time so you'll need a startup or accelerator payment to cover the other 9 months. Once that payment goes through, you can drop the accelerator payment because the clock will reset. In 12 months' time, you'll have built up enough money in the account to cover that next payment)*

Progress Notes & Savings Tracker:

Savings Tracker

Review Your Discretionary Spending

Current Spend	Annual Total	Revised Amount	Annual Saving

Review Your Fixed Expenses

Bill	Current Supplier	Cost	Annual Total	New Supplier	New Cost	Annual Saving

Debts Review

Debt	Owing	Lender	Interest Rate	Fee	New Lender	New Rate	New Fee	Savings

Business Expenses Review

Items	Current Spend	Annual Total	Revised Amount	Annual Savings

G IS FOR GET CLEAR

ONE priority at a time

"Focus is Power" ~ *Miriam Castilla*

It's time to focus on your WEALTH bucket. This bucket includes all debts, savings and investment funds.

This is where compound interest is either working for you or against you.

It's your job to swing that pendulum so more of your money starts working for you, leveraging the magic of compound interest.

Let's talk goals:

Like most people, I'm sure your BIG goal is to retire on an exotic beach somewhere with a cocktail in your hand, while your money is multiplying on autopilot (making money babies).

That's AWESOME, but getting there is easier and more do-able if you break it down into baby steps and focus on one at a time.

The smaller the baby steps, the better. Most people try to achieve too many things at once and end up going nowhere fast!

The key is to FOCUS on ONE baby step at a time.

Focus is Power.

Just like a laser beam cuts through diamonds because of its intense focus, your energy and resources will take you further faster, if you focus single-mindedly on one small step at a time.

And then the next... and the next

I know you want to save money AND pay off debt AND go on a holiday, but if you try doing all 3 at once, it'll take forever.

By focusing on just one baby step at a time, you'll enjoy the satisfaction of continual progress, achieve ALL your goals faster

AND become more magnetic to money in the process!

Because when you focus intensely on one thing, something magical happens. It's like the Universe comes to your aid in a gazillion unexpected ways to help it manifest.

Break bigger goals into smaller micro goals, so that at any point in time, you're focusing on just ONE of those micro goals.

We'll refer to this micro-goal as your current No.1 priority.

For example, say you want to save $20,000 cash and pay off a $10,00 credit card. You can break that down into micro-goals and mix them up like this:

1. save $2,000
2. pay $2,000 off the card
3. save another $3,000
4. pay $3,000 off the card
. etc

At any moment in time, you only have ONE FOCUS. This is the key to getting traction and building momentum.

Every time you tick off a micro-goal, you're rewarded with a rush of dopamine and endorphins. This will help you feel empowered and confident about your finances, shift your mindset and make you more magnetic.

It's great to have big plans and dreams. But breaking them down helps you achieve them faster and more frequently celebrate your progress.

Plus, each time you tick off a micro-goal, you get to take stock, reassess where you're at and choose the next micro-goal to lock it into your GPS.

Hitting Turbo Boost:

You'll achieve ALL your goals at lightning speed by:

1. applying any savings from the previous step towards your No.1 priority.

2. paying any & all surplus income directly towards it.

3. redirect ALL funds to the next goal once you've achieved this one.

Every time you clear a debt, be sure to add its minimum payment to the total pool of funds going towards the next goal.

All wealth funds stay in the wealth bucket & all surplus comes here.

I refer to this as 'tipping the cups' (some people call it the snowball technique). It's what helps you create momentum and leverage more and more compound interest.

As a result, each goal is achieved even faster, and your wealth creation accelerates over time.

The more disciplined you are with this, the sooner you'll be sitting on that beach, checking the cocktail list.

> **TOP TIP:** *Continue making only the MINIMUM PAYMENTS on debts that are not your current No.1 priority. By focusing all available funds towards ONE THING, you'll build momentum faster.*

How to choose your goals:

Everyone's goals and the order in which they achieve them will differ.

And you won't always choose the goal that makes the most mathematical sense. Because even more important than the numbers is your MINDSET and the way YOU FEEL about your finances, remember?

The better you feel about your finances and the more abundant your mindset, the more magnetic to money and opportunities you will be, which will help you achieve your goals faster!

So yes, look at what makes mathematical sense (such as paying off debts on the highest interest rates first). But always check into what makes you FEEL the most abundant.

(eg: paying back your mum might make you feel a lot better about yourself than paying off the credit card, even though mum isn't charging any interest. When you feel more in charge of your finances, your confidence grows, helping you show up confidently in your business and generate more income)

You want to feel great about your finances and proud of how you're managing them. So it's good to go for smaller wins first, build confidence, get momentum going and solidify this new way of life.

I do recommend EVERYONE makes a getting a decent emergency cash buffer in place a priority #becauselife.

Here is a list of things you might want to include in your goals list (that you can then break down into baby steps):

- Emergency cash buffer
- Pay off personal debt
- Save for home deposit
- Invest

- Boost retirement funds

- Pay off home loan

- Pay off investment loans

You'll be reviewing your list of micro-goals down the track, so don't overthink it too much. The important thing is to decide your current No.1 priority and start with that one micro-goal.

TOP TIP: *'Savings' is neither a goal nor a suitable name for a bank account. BE SPECIFIC! What are you saving for? A holiday? A retirement nest egg? An emergency fund? An investment fund? A home deposit?*

Remember:

"Clarity Precedes Success" ~ Robin Sharma

KEY POINTS:

- Your WEALTH bucket includes all debts, savings & investment funds.

- Break larger goals down into micro goals.

- Focus on ONE micro-goal at a time - this is your No.1 priority right now.

- All money stays in the wealth bucket & is redirected to the next priority.

ACTION STEPS:

1. List your financial goals in order of priority.

2. Break them down into micro goals.

3. Decide on your CURRENT NO.1 PRIORITY.

4. Apply all savings from the previous step towards this micro goal.

5. All surplus income (windfalls etc.) goes towards your No.1 priority.

6. Once a goal is achieved, all funds are directed to the NEXT micro-goal.

CASE STUDY

My story is that I "used to be good with money". I always had savings. I had a meticulous spreadsheet encapsulating all my family expenses and budget. I tracked when I put money in savings and why I took it out.

After I was made redundant, as a single mother with a toddler, everything stayed the same because I had a termination payment to keep me going.

However, once I started my business and had to start relying on inconsistent amounts and irregular frequency in my income from my business and support payments, it became really hard to track anything with any accuracy. I was in survival mode, both in managing my responsibilities as a mother and home-owner, and in my relationship with money.

The single most notable thing from Magnetic Money that started to shift things for me was 'making things easy'. This meant making choices aligned with me and my goals and values, even if they weren't what you were 'supposed to do', and learning how to stop attaching meaning to things going wrong.

And, just like that, money and opportunities started flowing more easily from clients and sources that make me feel valued rather than drained. And obstacles don't seem as insurmountable as they did before. I have a long way to go, but I can see my progress, and that makes me happy.

Romina Cavagnola
Alchemy of Alignment™ Publishing
www.facebook.com/alchemyofalignment/

Notes:

My Current No.1 financial goal:

Notes re my financial goals & priorities:

Breaking it down into micro-goals:

N IS FOR NEW TARGET

Define your baseline income and magic number

"Man aim at nothing, sure to hit it"
~ Confucius

A quick story from a client we'll call Sue:

Sue's son was getting married in a few months. She'd been saving but was worried she wouldn't be able to contribute as much to the wedding as she wanted to.

When she sat down to calculate her magic number, she realized that her target was quite achievable.

So she relaxed, stopped worrying about it and went back to focusing on running her business and serving her clients.

When the wedding date came around, Sue realized she had saved way MORE than she intended to and was able not only to contribute to the wedding, but surprise her son and his new wife with a beautiful gift on top.

Hilariously, a short time later, Sue's daughter announced she would be getting married within a few months too!

****

Congratulations! You're making awesome progress.

Giving every dollar a job to do and a place to do it, gives you clarity and financial peace of mind. It nurtures an abundance mindset and helps you feel great about your money.

So far you have:

- set up your banking to match your buckets
- allocated income & expenses to correct buckets
- identified your expenses

- plugged the leaks and trimmed the fat
- identified your current No.1 financial priority
- redirected all liberated funds towards your no.1 goal

You now know where the money for each expense can be found, how much needs to be there and where to direct all surplus income to.

The aim is to have neither surplus nor deficit in your money plan.

You want every dollar at work, not sitting around looking confused, lost or bored.

So let's make sure it all balances, which means every dollar has a job.

Start with your BASELINE income.

If you're a salary or wage earner, use your guaranteed regular income.

If you're self-employed, use a conservative income based on your last 6 months' average.

IMPORTANT: Always calculate your pre-tax income targets (ie gross turnover) when self-employed. You can download a handy income target calculator HERE if you need.

Remember, this is just a starting point to ensure the basics are covered.

Any surplus income will always be directed towards your No.1 priority.

And if you're concerned about having shortfall months, don't worry! We'll talk about how to manage and smooth irregular income and make up any shortfall in later steps.

For now, just focus on covering your basic expenses.

This will help you figure out what your baseline income needs to be.

YOUR MAGIC NUMBER:

Once you have your baseline income target, you can play with your figures and come up with your 'Magic Number'.

Your Magic number is simply the gap between where you'd like to be and your baseline.

It's that EXTRA income that will help you achieve your financial goals as quickly as you'd like to.

Example:

Your baseline income has you on target to save $20,000 in 20 months.

But you'd love to achieve that goal in just 10 months. This means you'd need an additional $1,000 personal income per month.

That's your Magic Number!

It helps you focus, set meaningful goals and make plans to achieve them.

What can you do to bring in that extra income? Do you need to get a payrise, a side hustle, raise your prices or create a new offer?

You get to choose!

And once that Magic Number has become your 'new normal' you reset your baseline and come up with a new Magic Number. **HOW FUN!!!**

> **TOP TIP:** *Your Magic Number should relate to your current micro-goal or the bigger goal it's part of. Else you'll confuse yourself and lose focus!*

KEY POINTS:

- 'Every dollar has a job to do' means zero surplus in your money planner.

- Base your money system on your baseline income. Include plenty of buffers and wiggle room.

- All surplus goes to your current No.1 priority.

ACTION STEPS:

1. Using your baseline income, 'balance the budget' so every dollar has a job to do.

2. Got surplus? Allocate it to your wealth bucket and your No.1 priority.

3. Got a shortfall? Revisit step A and make adjustments.

4. Once it balances, you're all set!

5. Now play with some Magic Numbers. What financial goals would you like to achieve? What income targets do they translate to? What can you do to bridge that gap?

CASE STUDY

As an Accountant, targets and goals are important to me.

So calculating a baseline income and magic numbers makes a lot of sense.

Once decided, the baseline income can be drawn down consistently to give a steady income flow.

This makes it easy to then look at the magic number – ie the TURNOVER you need in your business and the actions needed to generate it .

Remember, all of the planning and preparation in the world will not in itself generate Turnover, but once you know the magic number you can send that into the Universe and it will respond!

Karen Conlon
CEO, FCPA
https://sumtotalab.com.au/

Magnetic Money® Management System

Notes:

My Baseline Income Is:
_____
_____

My Current No.1 Priority Is:
_____
_____

On my baseline income, I'll achieve it by :
_____
_____

My Magic Number is:
_____
_____

My Magic Number will help me achieve the following goal/s in the following timeframes:
_____
_____
_____
_____

MORE NOTES:
_____
_____

E IS FOR EASY

Put your money system on autopilot

"Budgets Restrict, Systems Liberate"
~ Miriam Castilla

You're nearly there!

Money management is EASY when you make the effort to set up a system that you can trust to run on autopilot.

You've done the work.

Now it's time to switch to autopilot so you can sit back and relax!

You now KNOW the money to pay your bills will be there. So why spend time paying them manually? You have better things to do! (like enjoying your newfound freedom and abundance)

I do however recommend handing over the reins to automation slowly.

You've given every dollar a job to do so that your money can start working for you. But YOU still need to remember what you told it to.

You wouldn't buy a factory, hand out job descriptions, then walk out and never go back. You would keep an eye on things, making sure you know what's happening - especially in the early days. But you certainly don't need to walk the factory floor, micro-manage people or do their job for them!

It's the same with your money system. As your confidence and familiarity grows, you'll be able to step away more and more.

But the truth is, you might not want to! Because it's FUN to see the wheels of your money system turning. Watching your money going to work for you and making money babies is incredibly satisfying. It raises your vibe, makes you feel abundant and increases your money magnetism.

> **TOP TIP:** *If you have self-employed income, do NOT automate the transfer of tax money as that will vary with each income cycle as a percentage of gross turnover. We'll deal with this in step T.*

KEY POINTS:

- Automate internal transfers in stages as you build trust in your system.

- Continue looking over your bills to check that charges are correct.

- Make a diary note to regularly review all expenses (eg every 1-2 years).

CASE STUDY

Before Magnetic Money I was lost in the world of shifting money back and forth – robbing Peter to pay Paul.

It was exhausting to say the least.

More so, it felt demoralizing to never have enough, counting the money in my hand, or checking the bank account before I checked out the groceries. I always felt like I was short.

I also rarely accepted invitations to join friends on outings, because not having the money to get there felt like just the start.

Now that I'm using automation alongside my Magnetic Money Planner, things are so much better!

 I put money aside without thinking. It just happens.

So now groceries, special invitations and events don't have to weigh heavy on my heart or mind.

I simply know that the money is there and available for the extras, like days out with the grandchildren, theater shows and purchasing things for myself because I choose to.

I'm joyfully abundant and confident that my old way of dealing with money and/or the lack of money is gone!

Jackie Lawson
Eema Says ...
https://eemasays.com/

ACTION STEPS:

1. Set up direct debits for regular bills.

2. Set up regular transfers between your bank accounts as required.

3. Keep an eye on things until you feel comfortable.

4. Then automate a little more if you can.

> **TOP TIP:** *Pay bills on the shortest payment cycle available to help smooth your cash flow – eg: pay electricity bills monthly rather than quarterly, as long as there's no additional cost.*

Notes:

Bills to be direct debited:

Transfers between my accounts:

More Notes:

T IS FOR TRACK

Distribute Income & Smooth Cash Flow

"Track Progress - Not Expenses!"
~ Miriam Castilla

If you do NOT have a business or a side hustle, you don't need this step! Just continue paying all bonus income and unexpected cash received towards your No.1 priority.

Since this system naturally makes you more magnetic to money, that may happen more often than you expect!

Sold the lawnmower? Do this step!

Got an unexpected inheritance? Do this step!

Won cash in the lottery? Do this step!

Got a tax refund? Do this step!

If you DO have a business or side hustle, this step is your LIFELINE!

With the Magnetic Money® Management System, there is no need to micromanage your money and constantly track your expenses.

It has you covered.

You do however need to regularly tally and distribute your income to smooth your cash flow and stay on track.

You will complete this step each income cycle – monthly, bi-monthly or weekly, whatever works best for you.

This is your 5 minutes of money management.

This is all the effort required once your system is in place. But it's absolutely essential that these 5 minutes become a total non-negotiable.

This is how you stop robbing future YOU and create financial stability and security for yourself and your family.

You'll find a handy income distribution calculator along with the income target calculator at this link

> **TOP TIP:** *Only spend money AFTER it's been processed and distributed via the process in this step.*

KEY POINTS:

- This step is only for business owners & those with irregular income.

- Complete this step each & every income cycle.

- Make this 5-minute process a non-negotiable.

- Shortfall is only temporary – but it MUST be tracked and paid back FIRST!

CASE STUDY

Even though I procrastinated for the longest time, when I finally did it, setting up my buckets and different accounts made such a difference. I can't believe I put it off for so long!

But tracking the surplus and shortfall was a real gamechanger.

Before this there was a lack of clarity. I would think, "fingers crossed and hope it all works out!'

As an entrepreneur with an income that can vary from month to month, I love the peace of mind that comes with tracking the surplus and shortfall.

You know exactly where things stand.

And it's so much easier to have a gorgeous high abundance vibe now that the uncertainty and anxiety that always used to be lurking just below the surface has disappeared.

It's also so much easier for me to make informed financial and strategic decisions, such as whether I can work with a practitioner I want to work with or whether I need to just wait until the shortfall has been cleared.

Claire Kerslake
EFT Practitioner
www.clairekerslake.com

ACTION STEPS:

1. Add up all income for this period.

2. Calculate how much tax to put aside for self-employed income as a percentage of gross income.

3. Make personal income to buckets and accounts as required (*ie all that are NOT automated*) as per your money plan.

4. Got shortfall? Decide which account will be left short and make a note.

5. Got surplus? Make up any shortfall carried forward FIRST. Then pay the rest towards your No.1 priority!

TOP TIP: *If you have shortfall, it's usually easiest to leave your tax account short as your tax commitment is only due once a year, giving you plenty of time to make up the shortfall again.*

Notes:

I IS FOR ITERATE

Reset Your Goals As You Achieve Them

"Whatever you do, you have to keep moving forward" ~ Martin Luther King

What happens once you achieve your current No.1 priority?

You simply circle back and choose your next one!

What will your new No.1 priority be?

Once you decide, you program your autopilot with that new destination.

Here's the best bit:

Because you continue to keep all funds in the WEALTH bucket, you'll have more money available for that next goal – which means you'll get there even faster!

You start to build MOMENTUM.

It's a beautiful and powerful thing

KEY POINTS:

- Stick to the plan & ALWAYS have a No.1 priority.
- Keep ALL the money in your Wealth Bucket.
- When you iterate, take a moment to reconnect to your big WHY.

CASE STUDY

I was always praised for being organized. I'm quite focused, I have excellent self-discipline, and seeing the big picture was never a problem for me.

Until it came to money.

I would just spend it. I never had surplus money. I earned enough, and I would put a little here and there into retirement savings and towards travel. But I still ended up in debt.

I borrowed from my family and I over-extended myself with courses and programs because I had a thirst for learning and self-improvement that kept me in a cycle of always being on the edge of more debt.

Then I went into business for myself – while building a new life in a foreign country.

And my husband and I nearly lost it all.

When I joined Magnetic Money, we had already tried several blogs, courses, programs and coaches.

Up until Magnetic Money, every other tool we tried just didn't work for our situation because my income was so inconsistent.

That first step of mapping out our buckets was such a clear way to be certain of where all the money had to go – ESPECIALLY when we had financial obligations in two countries!

Working my way through the program on repeat has been a wonderful way to refine the systems that we first set up all those years ago. And we always start with the buckets.

We have paid off credit cards and vehicles. Our current bucket system is what keeps our household running, thankfully now in just one country.

The Map it Out section is the FOUNDATION of the Magnetic Money Process. It is the foundation of your new relationship with money.

And each year when I revisit this section, I get to celebrate the growth in my relationship with money and the growth in my net worth.

It's Magic!

Jen Lang
Voice Development and Spiritual Mentor
https://www.jenlang.com

ACTION STEPS:

1. Go back to G and define your new No.1 priority.

    G – Get Clear:

    - What should your next micro goal be?

    - Decide and define it.

2. Then move through steps N & E and make adjustments.

    N – New Target:

    - Allocate the money you were putting towards the previous priority towards your new one.

    - If you cleared a debt, take the minimum payment with you.

    - Review and adjust your figures.

    E – Make It Easy:

    - Adjust any automated transfers & payments as required.

3. Continue with step T as per usual.

   T – Track:

   - Continue tracking as before.

   - All surplus now goes to the NEW No.1 priority.

4. When you achieve this new micro-goal, ITERATE again!

> **TOP TIP:** *Remember to keep all funds in the wealth bucket. You're simply redirecting your fire hose to the next target.*

Notes:

Magnetic Money® Management System

C IS FOR CELEBRATE

Boost your money magnetism

"What you focus on, expands"

~ Someone Clever

This step is CRUCIAL!

Some people will be tempted to skip this step and just keep plugging away.

And look, it's great that you're so keen to keep going , but you'll miss out on a massive opportunity to become more magnetic – plus a whole lot of fun!

We call this the MAGNETIC Money® Management System for a reason!

Because we manage our money in ways that make us magnetic to more – by raising our vibration, increasing our joy and confidence levels by transforming our money mindset into one of abundance, certainty and TRUST.

Celebrating and acknowledging your progress is a massive part of that.

Just as you need regular work breaks to hit reset and keep life in balance, it's important to take a break and reward yourself for all the great work you've been doing with your money management.

In this step, you get to press pause and use the extra money you've been putting towards that no.1 priority on a rewarding treat for yourself.

THEN you can get stuck in again and direct those funds to your new no.1 priority.

> **TOP TIP**: *Decide on your celebrations upfront! It makes it easier at the time & helps you follow through*!

KEY POINTS:

- Rewarding and celebrating your achievements helps you stay motivated and inspired.
- Enjoying spending money on yourself helps you create a healthier relationship with money.
- FEELING ABUNDANT makes you magnetic!

ACTION STEPS:

1. Take a month off. Keep up only the minimum payments on financial commitments this month.
2. Take the EXTRA funds you were putting towards the No.1 priority you just ticked off and TREAT YOURSELF with it!
3. Make sure you really enjoy this and celebrate your progress.
4. The following month, direct those extra funds towards your new No.1 priority.

CASE STUDY

Need some inspiration on how to celebrate your milestones?

Here are some ideas from Magnetic Money® Club members:

- Celebrate paying off all debts (except our home loan) with a trip to Turkey & Egypt

- Celebrate paying back my sister by taking her out to lunch

- Celebrate clearing my student loans by buying myself a new bedroom suite

- Celebrate $10,000 in investment funds with a luxurious weekend away

- Celebrate paying the first $1,000 off my credit card by going camping for a week

- Celebrate paying off my car loan with a new handbag (bought on sale, of course!)

- Celebrate paying off our mortgage with a family trip to Europe

- Celebrate reaching $1million in retirement funds with a first class trip to LA

- Celebrate closing my credit card with a dinner at my favorite restaurant

How Will You Celebrate Achieving Your Goals?

Goal	Monthly Extras $	I will Celebrate By...

Notes:

Part 3

Create a truly rich life

YOUR MONEY SYSTEM IN ACTION

CONGRATULATIONS!!!

Getting your system in place takes some initial effort and commitment.

But we call this the **5-minute** Magnetic Money® Management System for a reason!

Because now that everything is up and running, managing your money will only take 5 minutes a week.

From here, you simply need to focus on step T, tracking your business income, taking note of any shortfall or surplus and distributing funds into your buckets until you achieve your current No.1 priority.

Then you celebrate & iterate.

THAT'S IT!

And if you don't have a business, you only need to worry about distributing any bonus income to that No.1 priority, then celebrating your milestones before you iterate and focus on the next micro-goal.

Step E – making it easy through automation will cut down the time you need to spend on this. As your confidence in your system grows, you'll be able to automate more and more.

Over time, you'll gather momentum, and those milestones will start dropping in faster and faster. Before you know it, you'll be in a completely different financial position to when you started.

Your life will change in magical ways.

That's why this is so worth doing!

A reminder:

If you ever find yourself needing motivation or inspiration, just look back at your notes about your big WHY and read over the case studies I share throughout this book.

If you'd like some personal support, the next page contains a list of resources you can tap into.

Have a beautiful day and once again – well done!!

I'm so happy you decided to commit to creating a richer, more abundant life for yourself, your family and your community.

xx Miriam

Magnetic Money® Management System

NEXT STEPS

Would you like more support with implementing your Magnetic Money® Management System?

Here are your options:

SELF STUDY: Magnetic Money® Management Bootcamp

Get instant access to the recordings of this live workshop series where I walk you through how to set up your system in detail and answer live participants' questions. Includes free access to future training calls: www.miriamcastilla.com/bootcamp

Magnetic Money® Management System

GROUP COACHING: The Magnetic Money® Club

Magnetic MONEY CLUB
Create A Truly RICH Life

Join our vibrant community and membership where we implement the Magnetic Money® Code. Includes live coaching and mentoring as well as custom hypnotic processes to facilitate rapid mindset transformation.

Find out more at

www.miriamcastilla.com/magnetic-money

Interested in becoming a Magnetic Money® Certified Coach?

MAGNETIC MONEY®
CERTIFIED COACH

Find out more at

www.miriamcastilla.com/mmca

Magnetic Money® Management System

ABOUT THE AUTHOR

Miriam Castilla

Money Coach, Author, Speaker, Mentor, Finance Adviser, Hypnotherapist

Dip Fin Services (MB), Evolve Certified Hypnotherapist, B.Eng (Chem), Certified Infinite Possibilities Trainer, Certified Ho'oponopono Practitioner, Timeline & NLP Practitioner

Miriam Castilla is a Money & Abundance Coach, an experienced Finance Professional and Hypnotherapist.

She also has a background in Engineering and Corporate

Development, having managed assets worth hundreds of millions of dollars.

Miriam left the corporate world and started her finance business after a divorce that left her struggling financially while caring for her two young children.

Within 3 years, she had built an award winning business, a multiple 6-figure income and purchased 3 properties.

Miriam is a bestselling author, international keynote speaker and has served as a mentor to young entrepreneurs through Flinders University's Venture Dorm program, supporting emerging businesses as both a director and investor.

Miriam has worked with a long list of Australian and International companies and featured in numerous publications.

She is a proud Infinite Possibilities Trainer and member of the TUT team, working with Mike Dooley (*of 'Notes from the Universe' & 'The Secret'*) to share the message that we are the creators of our lives, and our thoughts are all powerful.

Miriam's mission is to liberate small business owners from money stress and money shame, so they can embrace their value and make a meaningful impact with their work.

She takes a holistic approach to money, 'marrying the magical with the practical' to help you create a state of internal and external abundance.

As founder of the Magnetic Money® Coaching Academy and the Magnetic Money® Club, she shows business owners how to smooth irregular cash flow and achieve their financial goals by implementing a simple money management system.

This, combined with custom hypnotic processes to transform old money stories and beliefs as well as simple, powerful practices to energetically align with abundance is the secret to becoming magnetic and creating a truly rich life – inside and out.

Miriam and her husband Martin happily live in sunny Adelaide, South Australia, surrounded by their three adult children.

Magnetic Money® Management System

RESOURCES

A quick reminder about these free resources:

Grab Your Implementation Checklist at
www.miriamcastilla.com/checklist

Download Your Handy Calculators at
www.miriamcastilla.com/calculators

Free Workshop to Help You Organize Your Banking:
www.miriamcastilla.com/freeworkshop

Printed in Great Britain
by Amazon

41932599R00082